Newbridge Discovery Links®

Good Sports

Richard Merchant

Newbridge

A Haights Cross Communications ▶◀ ....pany

Good Sports
ISBN: 1-4007-3679-X

Program Author: Dr. Brenda Parkes, Literacy Expert

Written by Richard Merchant
Design assistance by Kirchoff/Wohlberg, Inc.

Newbridge Educational Publishing
11 East 26th Street, New York, NY 10010
www.newbridgeonline.com

Copyright © 2003 Newbridge Educational Publishing,
a Haights Cross Communications Company

Cover photograph: Venus and Serena Williams after winning the gold medal in women's doubles tennis at
the 2000 Olympic Games in Sydney, Australia.
Table of Contents photograph: Lance Armstrong competing in the 1999 Tour de France.

Photo Credits
Cover: AFP/Corbis; Table of Contents page: AP/Wide World Photos; page 4: AP/Wide World Photos;
page 5: (top) AP/Wide World Photos, (bottom) AP/Wide World Photos; page 6: Paul Harris/Getty Images;
page 7: (left & right) Paul Harris/Getty Images; page 8: Brad Mangin/Sports Illustrated; page 9: Action
Images/Icon SMI; page 10: Manny Milan/SI/Icon SMI; page 11: Kevin Lamarque/Reuters/TimePix;
page 12: AP/Wide World Photos; page 13: Manny Milan/Icon SMI; page 14: AP/Wide World Photos;
page 15: Erik Isakson/Icon SMI; page 16: AP/Wide World Photos; page 17: AP/Wide World Photos;
page 18: Wally McNamee/Corbis; page 19: Rick Stewart/Getty Images; page 20: AP/Wide World Photos;
page 21: AP/Wide World Photos; page 22: Mike Powell/Getty Images; page 23: AP/Wide World Photos;
page 24: AP/Wide World Photos; page 25: AP/Wide World Photos; page 26: AP/Wide World Photos;
page 27: AP/Wide World Photos; page 28: AP/Wide World Photos; page 29: AP/Wide World Photos;
page 30: Erik Isakson/Icon SMI

10 9 8 7 6 5 4 3 2

GUIDED READING	Guided Reading levels assigned by Newbridge, using the text characteristics
LEVEL **Q**	described by Fountas and Pinnell in *Guided Reading* (Heinemann, 1996).

Table of Contents

The Spirit of Great Athletes

Great athletes in action are exciting to watch. It's a thrill to see a skier fly down a steep, icy slope or to watch a tennis ball hurtle back and forth across the net as two top players compete.

What can make watching a sport even more thrilling is knowing what it took for a talented athlete to reach the top. Some athletes have overcome tremendous **obstacles.** Some have battled pain or serious illness. Talent wasn't enough for these men and women. Without **determination,** courage, and focus, they would never have become champions. They had to have spirit.

Practice Makes Perfect: The Williams Sisters

The Williams sisters' story begins in the 1980s. Richard and Oracene Williams and their five daughters were living in Compton, California. Venus and Serena were the youngest in the family.

Richard Williams always had big dreams for his daughters. After watching a tennis match on television, he decided his daughters could be tennis champions! They could lead exciting lives and make enough money to live comfortably when they grew up. In 1984, Richard began teaching Venus to play. She was only four years old! Serena started her lessons a year later.

Future tennis stars Venus (left) and Serena (right) with their father at the tennis courts in 1991.

Venus and Serena would practice for hours at a time at the tennis courts in Compton, California.

Most **professional** tennis players have experienced coaches and the best equipment, but the Williams family couldn't afford all that yet. Richard Williams made up his mind to give the girls their beginning lessons himself, even though he had never taken a tennis lesson. He had learned how to play from reading books and watching videos.

The Williamses couldn't afford to play at fancy tennis courts, either. The free public courts near their neighborhood were not in good shape. The pavement was cracked and broken and covered with **graffiti.**

Still, every day, Richard Williams packed six tennis rackets and seven milk crates filled with tennis balls into his car and drove Venus to the tennis court to practice.

Venus played her first professional tennis match when she was 14 years old.

Richard Williams took Venus to the courts day after day, week after week, to play. Each day, Richard threw hundreds of balls to Venus. At first, she missed a lot of the balls her father tossed her. But she kept trying and practicing and, eventually, she began to improve. By the time she was eight, she was winning **matches** in the junior tennis leagues. She was sure that she was going to be the best tennis player in the world. Venus was unstoppable.

Her little sister Serena was also learning to play by this time. Serena was good. And she was determined to play as well as her big sister.

Would these girls grow up to achieve greatness? Would all their practice and hard work pay off?

To answer that question, just imagine that you could have been present at the Lipton Championships tennis **tournament** on March 29, 1999, in Key Biscayne, Florida. It's the final match between the top two female tennis players. On one side of the net, standing 6'2", is . . .Venus Williams! She is now 18 years old. She's won every single match she's played in the tournament to get to this point.

Now, only one person stands between her and victory. Guess who it is?

Venus is known as a powerful tennis player. Her serve was clocked at 127 miles per hour. That set a world's record.

On the other side of the net, standing 5'10", is . . .Serena! Like Venus, Serena has not lost a single match in this tournament. Now, she has to play her own sister—in a match that will be seen on television around the world!

This is the first time the sisters have met in the final match of a major tennis tournament. Venus and Serena had played each other in competitions twice before. Venus, slightly older, won both matches. Now Serena is on a 16-game winning streak. She's caught up to her big sister.

Venus and Serena make a great team when they play as partners in doubles tennis. They won gold medals in the 2000 Sydney Olympics.

In 2002, the Williams sisters were the top-ranked women players in the world. Serena was ranked number one!

Imagine being Venus or Serena. It's hard to compete with your sister. You want to win. But if you win, your sister loses. And when you lose, it's hard not to be jealous. It's amazing that the Williams sisters have always managed to be good sports ever since they played each other as little girls.

In this match, Serena doesn't play her best, and Venus is the winner. After it's over, the sisters hug like best friends. As Serena said: "Family comes first, no matter how many times we play each other. Nothing will come between me and my sister."

All in the Family: The Alou Brothers

The Alou brothers hold the record for family togetherness in baseball. The three brothers came from the Dominican Republic. Felipe, the oldest, was the first to play on an American major-league team. Matty, the middle brother, moved up to the major leagues next. Jesus, the youngest, joined the major leagues in 1963.

Now, here's the surprising part. For one season, the Alou brothers all played for the San Francisco Giants.

But wait—it gets better. During one game, all three brothers played in the outfield. In left field was Matty. In center field was Felipe. In right field was Jesus. This is the only instance of an all-brother outfield in major-league history!

The Alou family tradition continues today. Felipe's son, Moises, is now a baseball star!

Big Dreams:
The Jamaican Bobsled Team

At first, people treated the idea as a joke. A bobsled team from Jamaica? Athletes from a tropical island in the Caribbean competing in a sport that requires snow and ice? But by the end of the 1988 Winter Olympic Games in Calgary, the Jamaican bobsled team had gone from being everyone's favorite joke to everyone's favorite Olympic story.

In 1988, Jamaica sent athletes to the Winter Olympic Games for the first time.

In bobsledding, teams of two or four race down a steep, icy course in a sled with steel **runners.** At the top of the hill, the team starts running down the course, pushing the sled in front of them. The "push-off" is the most important part of the race—getting off to a fast start. Then the runners quickly jump into the moving sled. The driver steers the sled around the sharp curves and **hairpin** turns on the course.

Bobsledding is popular in countries like Germany and Switzerland, where there is plenty of snow and ice. But how did the sport of bobsledding find its way to a tropical island, where snow never falls?

SALT LAKE 2002

OLYMPIC WINTER GAMES

Sleds reach speeds of 85 miles per hour. An Olympic bobsled team might finish a 1,500-meter course in about three minutes.

Devon Harris competed in three Olympic Games. Today, when he speaks to students, he tells them, "Sometimes you give up when you are so close to your dream, when just a little bit more effort would make the difference. That is why you should try harder and never give up."

The offbeat idea was suggested by two businessmen. Some people who worked in the Jamaican Defense Force, which is Jamaica's military organization, liked the idea and got the team started.

Six Jamaican men who wanted a chance to compete in the Olympics tried out for the team and made it. The Jamaican bobsled team was born! The team members' names were Devon Harris, Dudley Stokes, Michael White, Freddie Powell, Clayton Soloman, and Caswell Allen.

Some of the teammates had competed in track-and-field events and had tried out for the Jamaican Olympic team as sprinters. They hadn't made the team but their talent and training as sprinters could help them with the all-important push-off in a bobsled race.

Bobsled teams use pushcarts like this one to train for competition.

Under the leadership of their captain, Dudley Stokes, the team began their training by racing pushcarts on the hills of Jamaica. That winter, they headed north and started practicing on real bobsled tracks. In the winter of 1988, they arrived in Calgary, Canada, ready to compete in the Olympic Games.

Who Invented the Bobsled?

The sport of bobsledding has roots in both the United States and Europe. In the 1880s, racing lumbersleds was a popular sport in Albany, New York. In 1888, the first sled with steel runners was introduced in St. Moritz, a ski village in Switzerland. A four-man bobsled competition was held in 1924 at the very first Winter Olympic Games in Chamonix, France. The first women's bobsled teams competed in the 2002 Salt Lake City Olympics.

That year, the Jamaicans crashed halfway down the trail. Nonetheless, they refused to give up. They won the hearts of fans by picking up their sled and carrying it to the finish line!

Since their first Olympics, the Jamaican team has shown that they are serious about their sport. By the 1994 Olympics, the team had gotten much better. In the four-man bobsled competition, the team finished in 14th place, ahead of both teams from the United States.

A team from Jamaica has participated in every winter Olympics since 1988. The story of Jamaican bobsledding goes to show what really determined athletes can do!

Members of the Jamaican bobsled team trained in Evanston, Wyoming. To earn money for the 1998 Games, the teammates worked in the local pizza parlor, making and delivering pizza.

Getting in the Game: Manon Rheaume

On September 23, 1992, Manon Rheaume made sports history. She became the first woman to play on a professional major-league sports team. And Manon broke into one of the roughest men's sports of them all: professional ice hockey.

During an **exhibition** game for the National Hockey League (NHL), the Tampa Bay Lightning put Manon in the goalkeeper position. It's the goalkeeper's job to keep the opposing team from scoring. Would she survive out there on the ice?

This goalkeeper not only survived, she excelled! Manon stopped seven out of nine goal attempts during that game.

Goaltending is one of the toughest positions to play in hockey. Goalies must stay focused for the entire game.

Manon was a member of the Canadian women's hockey team during the 1998 Olympic Games in Nagano. The team took home silver medals.

For people who knew Manon, her NHL moment was no surprise. She had been playing ice hockey in her hometown in Quebec, Canada, since she was five years old. Her brothers all played hockey and Manon learned to be a goalkeeper by guarding the net against her brother's practice shots.

At six, she played her first official game when her father, who coached an all-boys' team, needed a replacement player. Throughout her childhood, Manon continued to play on boys' teams because there weren't many opportunities for girls to play hockey. Manon loved the game and wanted to play.

At 11, Manon became the first girl to play in the International Pee Wee Hockey Tournament in Canada. Today, there are hockey leagues just for girls.

As she said after her first game in the major leagues, "I didn't try to be the first woman to do this, I just want to play . . . I love hockey and want to go higher. It's a passion for me."

Both before and after her 1992 NHL **debut**, Manon continued to play on **amateur** and semiprofessional men's teams. She also played in the 1992 and 1994 World Women's Hockey Championships and in the 1998 Olympic Games.

Manon's love for ice hockey helped her break new barriers and show the world what she could do. As she said, "It's never been easy. But I've always wanted to play hockey. If you have that kind of desire, I think you can achieve what you want to achieve." Manon's words are an inspiration for all athletes—and for everyone!

At the Top of the Hill: Picabo Street

This female Olympic star might be as famous for her name as she is for her skiing. The first time most people heard of Picabo (pronounced "peek-a-boo") Street was in 1994. The United States, not famous for its Olympic skiing champions, sent Picabo to the 1994 Olympics. Though she was unknown to most people, Picabo shocked the world by winning a silver medal!

In the next two years, she went on to win the 1995 and 1996 World Cup skiing contests.

Picabo learned to ski when she was six years old. She made the Olympic ski team for the first time when she was only 17 years old.

Would Picabo be able to come back from her injuries?

Then, in December 1996, something awful happened. Picabo was training in Vail, Colorado. As she was speeding down the ski trail, she hit a smooth spot where she usually hit a bump.

Picabo knew she was going to crash. Instead of panicking, she did some really fast thinking. She knew that if she turned her skis one way she would injure both knees. She would never make it back to the Olympics.

So, Picabo made the instant decision to crash a different way, and injure only her left knee. In a split second, going 70 miles per hour, she figured all this out. Then—SMACK!— she crashed. She tore a **ligament** in her left knee. Surgery and **rehabilitation** to repair the knee kept Picabo off skis for more than six months.

In July 1997, Picabo got back on skis for the first time. It was hard, painful work getting back in shape, but spending time away from the sport helped Picabo realize how much she loved it. She had missed the sensation of flying down a mountain.

In February 1998, Picabo was again standing at the top of the ski slope—at the 1998 Winter Olympics in Nagano, Japan! Through hard work and belief in herself, Picabo made an amazing recovery. Now was her real moment of truth. Could she still ski just as well? Would she get hurt again?

Picabo Street amazed everyone. She won the gold medal!

Downhill skiing is a tough sport and it takes courage just to compete. As Picabo says, "When you're screaming down the mountain and one-hundredth of a second is what separates the first, second, and third person, everybody's a winner."

A True Champion: Lance Armstrong

People always considered Lance Armstrong a great athlete. But when he was able to come back from a devastating illness to win one of cycling's greatest prizes, Armstrong became more than a champion. He became a sports legend, loved and admired for his courage and spirit as much as for his athletic skills.

When Lance Armstrong was a boy growing up in Plano, Texas, he loved sports. At the age of 13, he had won a children's triathlon. A triathlon is a competition with three parts, usually running, swimming, and cycling.

Lance was good enough to train with Olympic athletes when he was still in high school.

Lance was the winner in the 1995 and 1996 Tour DuPont races. The Tour DuPont is the biggest cycling race in the United States.

By the time he was in high school, cycling had become Lance's sport. Most cycling races are long-distance **marathons** and Lance used to bike for miles and miles to practice. On Saturdays, Lance would sometimes cycle, from his home in Plano, more than 50 miles to the Oklahoma border. In 1991, at the age of 20, he became America's national amateur cycling champion.

After turning professional, Lance started to show the racing world what he could do. In 1993, he won ten major cycling competitions. By 1996, he was ranked as the number-one cyclist in the world. It seemed that nothing could stop him.

Something did stop him, though. It started when he felt unusually tired after winning the Tour DuPont in 1996. He wasn't performing as well in races. He wasn't riding as fast as he used to. Finally, he decided to go to a doctor.

At the doctor's office, Lance Armstrong discovered the frightening truth—he had cancer. Lance was only 25 years old and he didn't know if he would ever race again. Worse than that, he didn't know if he would even survive.

Lance credits his doctors and new advances in cancer treatment for his amazing recovery from cancer.

Every year Lance Armstrong's foundation sponsors the Ride for the Roses, a bike race that raises money for cancer research and cancer survivors.

Lance had a choice between two types of **treatment.** With one treatment, the chemicals used to fight the cancer would not make him feel sick, but they would damage his lungs permanently. This would mean that he might never cycle again. The other treatment might be very painful, but his lungs would not be affected. Lance courageously chose the second treatment, so that one day he might compete again. Lance had two operations, and many courses of cancer treatment. Finally, in early 1997, the cancer was gone. Lance was cured!

After beating cancer, Lance Armstrong believed he could do anything. In 1999, he was ready to compete in the Tour de France, an important bike race in France. Cyclists race in teams for this event, and no team wanted Lance. No one believed that someone who had been so sick could ever compete again. Finally, the United States Postal Service team was willing to take him on.

The Tour de France is the biggest and best cycling race—it's like the Super Bowl for cyclists. The course, which changes every year, takes cyclists on a 3,500-kilometer race that lasts for about three weeks and takes cyclists up and down steep mountain slopes.

The yellow jersey is a famous symbol of the Tour de France. Each day during the race, the leader gets to wear a yellow jersey.

When the Tour de France started on July 3, 1999, the competition was tough and Lance was not favored to win. But from the start of the race, Lance took the lead, and each day he continued to ride well. His win was a stunning victory.

Lance Armstrong went on to win three more Tour de France races! He also wrote a book about his experience and started a foundation to raise money for cancer survivors. His story gives hope to people fighting cancer and to athletes everywhere.

The Tour de France race ends in Paris. Riders race through the city before crossing the finish line.

The World's Greatest Bicycle Race

The first Tour de France was started because of a rivalry between two French sports newspapers. An editor of one of the newspapers, *L'Auto*, thought that a major sports race would get more people to read his newspaper. In 1903, he planned a bicycle race all through France that would last more than a month. The race, the Tour de France, was a huge success. It is even more popular today.

That's the Spirit

The athletes in this book have overcome all kinds of obstacles. Their spirit and determination have taken them from simple beginnings to championship tennis, from cart-racing in Jamaica to bobsledding in the Olympics, and from life-threatening illness to the finish line of the Tour de France. Their moments of triumph can inspire us all.

Glossary

amateur: an athlete who does not play for money

debut: the first appearance or beginning of a professional career

determination: the act of sticking to a purpose or a goal

exhibition: a game played for the public that is not part of a regular season

graffiti: markings or drawings that are written or spray-painted on sidewalks or walls

hairpin: sharply curved, as in a U-shaped turn

ligament: strong band of white tissue that connects bones to other bones or to cartilage

marathon: a race or game that lasts for an extremely long time

match: a game or contest in which two or more players play against each other

obstacle: something that gets in your way or prevents you from reaching a goal

professional: an athlete whose sport is an occupation and a way of earning money

rehabilitation: to bring back to a condition of good health

runners: thin metal blades on the bottom of a sled

tournament: a contest where many players compete against each other in a number of games

treatment: a set of medical procedures that are meant to heal or cure a person

Index

Websites

www.sikids.com
www.infoplease.com/sports.html